STOP

Believing in God!

Know Him

**The World Believes in all Manner of gods,
But We *Know* GOD**

Presented by Ellen Lefavour

STOP
Believing in God!

Know Him

The World Believes in all Manner of gods,
But We *Know* GOD

Printed in USA

First Edition July 2016

ISBN

978-0-9907737-6-4

For more information, visit:
www.hobbithousestudio.com
and please visit Blog: www.godsmorning.live

Presented by Ellen Lefavour
Hobbit House Studio
Gloucester, Massachusetts

Contents

Quotes

Habakkuk 2:14 "For the earth will be filled with the *knowledge* of the glory of the LORD, as the waters cover the sea."

Hosea 6:3 "So let us *know*, let us press on to *know* the Lord. His going forth is as certain as the dawn; And He will come to us like the rain, Like the spring rain watering the earth."

Isaiah 43:10-11 "You are My witnesses," says the LORD, 'And My servant whom I have chosen, That you may *know* and believe Me, And understand that I am He. Before Me there was no God formed, Nor shall there be after Me. I, even I, am the LORD, And besides Me there is no other.'"

1 John 2:3-4 "By this we *know* that we have come to *know* Him, if we keep His commandments. The one who says, 'I have come to know Him,' and does not keep His commandments, is a liar, and the truth is not in him;"

Jeremiah 9:23-24 "Thus says the Lord, 'Let not a wise man boast of his wisdom, and let not the mighty man boast of his might, let not a rich man boast of his riches; but let him who boasts boast of this, that he understands and *knows* Me, that I am the Lord who exercises loving kindness, justice and righteousness on earth; for I delight in these things,' declares the Lord."

Prelude

It suddenly struck me one day how many Christians seem to practice their faith based on what they *believe*, rather than *Who they know*. I began to wonder if it was just a matter of symantics, or if it went deeper and was more problematic than that.

What we believe can be fickle and changeable. I can look back over my life at many things I have believed, only to later find that they were untrue. The world is filled with *beliefs* that are founded on deception and lies. Our Christian walk should never be based on something as flimsy and changeable as belief. Satan can attack beliefs six ways to Sunday—just look at what he has done to religion!

Christianity is based on a relationship with God our Father, made possible through the redemptive power of Jesus Christ our Lord crucified and resurrected, and empowered by the Holy Spirit—persons we *know*, or should *know* personally and intimately. If we *know* them, we *know* them—there is no reason to say we *believe* in them. If we don't *know* them, we need to.

Based on scripture and the definitions of *believe* and *know*, this book takes us through the steps of how children of God come to personally and intimately *know* their Heavenly Father, and contrasts it with the children of the World, who *believe* all sorts of things that are founded on deceptions and lies because they do not and cannot know God. If we are Christ's, we have no business in the belief system of the World.

What we do believe is "every word that proceeds out of the mouth of God", *because we know Him*, and we *know* there is no deception in Him. The World on the other hand, is filled with deception and lies. Stop Believing in God - *Know Him.*

Chapter 1: Knowing vs. Believing

Knowing

"Now we have received, not the spirit of the world, but the Spirit who is from God, that we might **know** the things that have been freely given to us by God." 1 Corinthians 2:12

"Be still, and **know** that I am God; I will be exalted among the nations, I will be exalted in the earth." Psalm 46:10-11

Believing

"All the World is made up of faith and trust and pixie dust."
J.M. Barrie, Peter Pan

"I **believe** in God, but not as one thing, not as an old man in the sky. I **believe** that what people call God is something in all of us. I **believe** that what Jesus and Mohammed and Buddha and all the rest said was right. It's just that the translations have gone wrong." John Lennon

"Well, I **believe** life is a Zen koan, that is, an unsolvable riddle. But the contemplation of that riddle—even though it cannot be solved—is, in itself, transformative. And if the contemplation is of high enough quality, you can merge with the divine." Tom Robbins

Chapter 1: Believing Vs. Knowing

There are many Christian devotions, such as the Apostles Creed, hymns and contemporary songs that include lines or lyrics such as: "I believe in God the Father, I believe in Christ the Son, I believe in the Holy Spirit…" I was singing one of them one day, and it suddenly struck me that it was wrong. I do not believe in God the Father, I do not believe in Christ the Son, I do not believe in the Holy Spirit—I *know* them, intimately and personally. I *know* them more intimately than anyone or anything in life.

There is a significant difference between believing and knowing something. We *know* the law of gravity exists; we *believe* the lights will come on when we flip the switch. When it comes to God, we do not accept Him as true, or hold an opinion, thought or supposition about Him—in faith we know Him—we *know* He is God Almighty, Creator of Heaven and Earth, and our Father. In faith, we *know* Jesus is our Best Friend, Brother, Redeemer and Lord; and we *know* the Holy Spirit is our Helper, Comforter, Guide, Gift-Giver and Fruit Bearer.

To *Believe* is to accept (something) as true—feel sure of the truth of; or to hold (something) as an opinion—think or suppose.
To *Know* is to be aware of through observation, inquiry, or information; or to have developed a relationship with (someone) through meeting and spending time with them; to be familiar or friendly with.
Faith is complete trust or confidence in someone or something. "Faith is the substance of things hoped for, the evidence of things not seen."

People who *know* God, *know* Him. We have a deep personal relationship with Him, we communicate with Him and He communicates with us (in

STOP Believing in God! Know Him

many different ways). We *know* Him through observation of His creation and how He manages and works in and through it. We *know* Him from personal inquiry and through His amazing answers. We *know* Him most informationally through His Word, the Bible—His autobiography—which tells us everything we need to know in order to *know* Him. We *know* Him most intimately through His Son, Jesus, who came so that we might *know* and be reconciled with Him. "I and the Father are one." "If you *know* me you will *know* the Father as well." "While we were enemies we were reconciled to God by the death of his Son."

In addition to knowing God intimately through Jesus, we also have complete faith in him. John 17:3 "This is eternal life, that they may *know* You, the only true God, and Jesus Christ whom You have sent." It all begins with faith, that we seek Him in the first place, which He has given us—He has set His eye on us, and given us a heart to *know* Him. Jeremiah 24:6-7 "For I will set My eyes on them for good, and I will bring them back to this land; I will build them and not pull them down, and I will plant them and not pluck them up. Then I will give them a heart to *know* Me, that I am the LORD; and they shall be My people, and I will be their God, for they shall return to Me with their whole heart." 1 Corinthians 2:12 "Now we have received, not the spirit of the world, but the Spirit who is from God, that we might *know* the things that have been freely given to us by God." He doesn't say to *believe* in Him—He says to *know* Him.

The World on the other hands, does not know God. 1 Corinthians 2:14 "But the natural man does not receive the gifts of the Spirit of God, for they are foolishness to him, and he cannot know them, because they are spiritually discerned." Trying to explain a relationship with God to the World is

Chapter 1: Believing Vs. Knowing

akin to trying to explain algebra to a cow; they are incapable of understanding—it is unintelligible gibberish to them because it requires discernment, which they lack.

As we are fully aware because were once of the World, it is only Spirit speaking to spirit that can ever open the door to knowing. And because "The wicked in his proud countenance does not seek God; God is in none of his thoughts…" his heart is hardened and his spirit is as though dead, although not dead, or there would be no enmity toward Christians by the World—they would just call us fools and pay us no mind. There is enough God consciousness in their spirits to convict them of their wickedness against God when they encounter His Spirit in us—worse still if we speak out about Him—that they feel guilty and if guilty enough, angry or even enraged. I can still remember hiding or running the other way when I saw my "hound of Heaven" uncle headed my way before I accepted Christ (I thank God for him being such a determined hound!).

The World at large is made up of believers. They **believe** in politics, government, the Federal Reserve, Wall Street, The System, their right to do as they please, the right to rewrite the Laws of God, global warming or climate change, all manner of gods and deities, and that "they" are the cause of their problems in life.

True Christians on the other hand **know**. We **know** God, we **know** that He is Sovereign, we **know** that we have been redeemed through Christ, we **know** that we are children of God—He is our Abba, Father—we **know** that nothing of the world can touch us because He is our refuge and shelter, our fortress and rock.

Chapter 2: God Is Not the Tooth Fairy

Jeremiah 16:19 "O LORD, my strength and my stronghold, and my refuge in the day of distress, to You the nations will come from the ends of the earth and say, '*Our fathers have inherited nothing but falsehood, futility and things of no profit.*'"

Psalm 40:4 "How blessed is the man who has made the LORD his trust, and has not turned to the proud, *nor to those who lapse into falsehood.*"

Chapter 2: God is Not the Tooth Fairy

The World is filled with so many nonsensical beliefs foisted upon us from the time we are little children, that it is not surprising the children of the World grow up to become such easily fooled adults. We start out being led to believe—by our own parents, the ones we look to for our information about the reality of life—in the tooth fairy, Santa Claus, the Easter Bunny, dragons, fairies, leprechauns, unicorns, etc.

If these imaginary beings are introduced on top of a solid foundation of the knowledge of God, and identified as whimsical fantasy creatures or fairy tales, I suppose they are harmless enough. If they are introduced in lieu of the knowledge of God, our foolishness and gullibility has been firmly established at a young age, and Satan's job has been made easy.

One day we realize the truth that the tooth fairy, Santa Claus, Easter Bunny, dragons, fairies, leprechauns and unicorns are not real, and we are disappointed, sad, maybe even a little angry—our programmed belief system has been threatened—we can no longer even believe our creator parents; however we keep searching for something to believe in. The children of the World, have been established at that young, impressionable age, to *believe* in fantasy, to *believe* lies, and unless they come to *know* the true and living God at some point, they spend the rest of their lives seeking after dangerous fantasy beings, as they once sought dragons and unicorns.

The children of the World then grow up to be adults easily led to *believe* in goddesses, all manner of deities, gurus, charlatans, humanism, government as provider, politicians as friends, the military as protection, banks and investment firms as security, one-world government and religion as good, and lies as truth. Satan is behind all these seemingly harmless and enchanting deceptions, and he is really good at what he does.

Psalm 4:2 "O sons of men, how long will my honor become a reproach? How long will you love what is worthless and aim at deception?"

Jeremiah 13:25 "This is your lot, the portion measured to you from Me," declares the LORD, 'because you have forgotten Me and trusted in falsehood.'"

Jeremiah 16:19 "O LORD, my strength and my stronghold, and my refuge in the day of distress, to You the nations will come from the ends of the earth and say, 'Our fathers have inherited nothing but falsehood, futility and things of no profit.'"

Psalm 40:4 "How blessed is the man who has made the LORD his trust, and has not turned to the proud, nor to those who lapse into falsehood."

It is not surprising that many Christians who grew up with these fantasies rather than a solid foundation of the knowledge of God, likewise become believers in and dependent on the World system, rather than placing their complete trust in God. If we *believe* in God, Jesus and the Holy Spirit, then like Santa Claus, they could be proven to be untrue, so Satan whispers to us: "Best to keep all your options open and available to you—don't put all your eggs in one basket". It is only when we intimately *know* God, Jesus and the Holy Spirit that we are able to discern the fantasies of the World

Chapter 2: God is Not the Tooth Fairy

for what they are—lies and deceptions promoted by our enemy. So if you *believe* in God, stop it now, and *know* Him.

In John 17:3, Jesus prayed: "This is eternal life, that they may *know* You, the only true God, and Jesus Christ whom You have sent." If we have accepted the gift of eternal life through faith in Jesus Christ, we have come to *know* God; however, we need to come to *know* God far more deeply and intimately than we do—to keep seeking and searching the unsearchable Him to *know* more of the depths and wonders of Him.

After twenty plus years as a believer, the apostle Paul said that he had not yet attained to the surpassing worth of *knowing* Christ as he ought, but he pressed on toward that goal (Philippians 3:7-14). If that was true for Paul, who we can all agree was not your average follower of Christ, how much more true must it be for us! Hosea (6:3) "Let us *know*, let us press on to *know* the Lord; his going forth is sure as the dawn; he will come to us as the showers, as the spring rains that water the earth."—*know,* not *believe* in.

1 John 2:3-4 "By this we *know* that we have come to *know* Him, if we keep His commandments. The one who says, 'I have come to know Him,' and does not keep His commandments, is a liar, and the truth is not in him;"

If we are entrenched in the World, following its gods and idols, we are not keeping His commandments, and cannot *know* Him.

Chapter 3: Knowing God Informationally

Proverbs 2:1-9 "My son, if you receive my words, And treasure my commands within you, so that you incline your ear to wisdom, and apply your heart to understanding; yes, if you cry out for discernment, and lift up your voice for understanding, if you seek her as silver, and search for her as for hidden treasures; then you will understand the fear of the LORD, and find the *knowledge* of God. For the LORD gives wisdom; from His mouth come *knowledge* and understanding; he stores up sound wisdom for the upright; he is a shield to those who walk uprightly; he guards the paths of justice, and preserves the way of His saints. Then you will understand righteousness and justice, equity and every good path."

Matthew 22:29 "But Jesus answered them, 'You are wrong, because you *know* neither the Scriptures nor the power of God.'"

Chapter 3: Knowing God Informationally

From the Bible (God's autobiography), we know that the attributes and characteristics of God are:

Wisdom: He has the ability to devise perfect ends and to achieve these ends by the most perfect means. God makes no mistakes. Romans 11:33-34 "O the depth of the riches and wisdom and *knowledge* of God! How unsearchable are His judgments and inscrutable His ways! For who has known the mind of the Lord, or who has been His counselor?"

Infinitude: God is infinite—He knows no boundaries. He is without measure. Since God is infinite, everything about Him is infinite. Psalm 145:3 "Great is the LORD, and highly to be praised, And His greatness is unsearchable."

Sovereignty: God rules His entire creation and is in control of everything that happens. Being all-knowing and all-powerful allows Him absolute freedom to do whatever He knows to be best. Although God is sovereign, He gave man free will to make and be responsible for his choices in life. Our most important choice in life is whether or not we choose to *know* and honor Him—every other choice in life is ultimately of no significance.

Holiness: God's Holiness—His majesty and His perfect moral purity—sets Him apart, further than east is from west, from all His created beings. There is absolutely no sin or evil thought in God. He is the definition of what is pure and righteous in the universe. Deuteronomy 32:4 "The Rock! His work is perfect, For all His ways are just; A God of faithfulness and without injustice, Righteous and upright is He."

STOP Believing in God! Know Him

Immutability: God never changes.

Trinity: The Father, Son, and Holy Spirit are all called God, worshipped as God, exist eternally yet are completely intermingled, and are involved in doing things only God could do. Although God reveals Himself in three persons, God is indivisible, and All are completely involved whenever One of the Three is active. John 16:13 "But when he, the Spirit of truth, comes, he will guide you into all the truth. He will not speak on his own; he will speak only what he hears, and he will tell you what is yet to come." John 8:42 "Jesus said to them, 'If God were your Father, you would love me, for I have come here from God. I have not come on my own; God sent me.'"

Faithfulness: Everything that God has promised will come to pass. He cannot lie. All He has said about Himself in His autobiography is true.

Love: Love is such an important aspect of God's character that the apostle John wrote, "God is love." God holds the well-being of others as His primary concern. To see His love in action, we study the life of Jesus—His sacrifice on the cross for our sins was the ultimate act of love. God's love is given freely and abundantly to the objects of His affection—those who choose to follow His Son Jesus, and are now His adopted children.

1 Corinthians 13 "Though I speak with the tongues of men and of angels, but have not love, I have become sounding brass or a clanging cymbal. And though I have the gift of prophecy, and understand all mysteries and all knowledge, and though I have all faith, so that I could remove mountains, but have not love, I am nothing. And though I bestow all my goods

Chapter 3: Knowing God Informationally

to feed the poor, and though I give my body to be burned, but have not love, it profits me nothing. Love suffers long and is kind; love does not envy; love does not parade itself, is not puffed up; does not behave rudely, does not seek its own, is not provoked, thinks no evil; does not rejoice in iniquity, but rejoices in the truth; bears all things, believes all things, hopes all things, endures all things.

Love never fails. But whether there are prophecies, they will fail; whether there are tongues, they will cease; whether there is knowledge, it will vanish away. For we know in part and we prophesy in part. But when that which is perfect has come, then that which is in part will be done away. When I was a child, I spoke as a child, I understood as a child, I thought as a child; but when I became a man, I put away childish things. For now we see in a mirror, dimly, but then face to face. Now I *know* in part, but then I shall *know* just as I also am *known*.

And now abide faith, hope, love, these three; but the greatest of these is love."

Self-existence: God has no beginning or end. He just is. The Bible says, "In the beginning, God created the heavens and the earth." He was there before the beginning.

Self-sufficiency: God has life in Himself. John 5:26 "For as the Father has life in Himself, so he has granted the Son also to have life in Himself,". All other life in the universe is a gift from God. He needs nothing, and there is nothing that can improve Him. He does not need our help with anything, but because of His grace and love, He allows us to be a part of advancing

STOP Believing in God! Know Him

His plan on earth by sharing His love with others, so they might come to *know* and glorify Him.

Eternal: God has always been and will forever be, because God dwells in eternity. Time is His creation, which is how he can see the end from the beginning, and can never be taken by surprise.

Goodness: God's attribute of goodness predisposes Him to be kind, compassionate, benevolent, and filled with good will toward men, and to bestow His many blessings on His children. God's actions define what goodness is, and are manifested in the flesh in the way Jesus related to the people around Him. Psalm 106:1 "Praise the LORD! Oh give thanks to the LORD, for He is good; for His lovingkindness is everlasting."

Gracious: God enjoys giving gifts to those who love Him, even when they do not deserve it—this is Grace. Jesus Christ is the channel through which His grace moves. John 1:17 "From His fullness we have all received grace upon grace. For the Law was given through Moses; grace and truth came through Jesus Christ."

Justice: God is just, and it is His character that defines what being just is. He, being just, brings moral equity to everyone. When there are evil acts, justice demands there be a penalty; however, because of His love, God paid the penalty for our evil deeds by going to the cross Himself. His justice needed to be satisfied, but He took care of it on behalf of all who accept His gift of grace through Jesus Christ.

Mercy: God is actively compassionate. Since God's justice is satisfied in Jesus, He freely shows mercy to all those who have chosen to follow Him.

Chapter 3: Knowing God Informationally

Since it is part of God's nature, His mercy will never end. For those who choose to despise or ignore God, His justice becomes His prominent attribute.

Omnipotence: God is "All-powerful". He is infinite and He possesses power, therefore He possesses infinite power. He allows His creatures to have some power, but it in no way diminishes His own. When the Bible says God rested on the seventh day, it was to set an example for us, not because He was tired—God never sleeps.

Omnipresence: God is "always present." Since God is infinite, His being knows no boundaries. The phrase "I am with you always" is repeated over twenty times in both the Old and New Testaments. Isaiah 41:10 "So do not fear, for I am with you; do not be dismayed, for I am your God. I will strengthen you and help you; I will uphold you with my righteous right hand." Matthew 28:20 "And surely I am with you always, to the very end of the age."

Omniscience: God is all-knowing—He knows everything, and His knowledge is infinite. We cannot hide anything from God. Jeremiah 23:24 "Can a man hide himself in hiding places so I do not see him? Declares the LORD, "Do I not fill the heavens and the earth?" Declares the LORD.

Psalm 139 1-16 "O LORD, You have searched me and known me. You know my sitting down and my rising up; You understand my thought afar off. You comprehend my path and my lying down, and are acquainted with all my ways. For there is not a word on my tongue, but behold, O LORD, You know it altogether. You have hedged me behind and before, and laid

STOP Believing in God! Know Him

Your hand upon me. Such *knowledge* is too wonderful for me; it is high, I cannot attain it.

Where can I go from Your Spirit? Or where can I flee from Your presence? If I ascend into heaven, You are there; If I make my bed in hell, behold, You are there. If I take the wings of the morning, and dwell in the uttermost parts of the sea, even there Your hand shall lead me, and Your right hand shall hold me. If I say, "Surely the darkness shall fall on me," even the night shall be light about me; indeed, the darkness shall not hide from You, but the night shines as the day; the darkness and the light are both alike to You.

For You formed my inward parts; You covered me in my mother's womb. I will praise You, for I am fearfully and wonderfully made; marvelous are Your works, and that my soul knows very well. My frame was not hidden from You, when I was made in secret, and skillfully wrought in the lowest parts of the earth. Your eyes saw my substance, being yet unformed. And in Your book they all were written, the days fashioned for me, when as yet there were none of them.

How precious also are Your thoughts to me, O God! How great is the sum of them! If I should count them, they would be more in number than the sand; When I awake, I am still with You."

We come to *know* God quite well by reading His Word; that is why He gave it to us. The more time we spend reading it, the more personally we *know* Him—the closer we draw to Him, and the closer He draws to us. James 4:8 "Draw near to God and He will draw near to you."

Chapter 4:
Knowing God
Through Observation

"WAS IT NOT MY HAND WHICH MADE ALL THESE THINGS?"
Acts 7:50

STOP Believing in God! Know Him

When we observe God's creation, we cannot help but come to **know** Him. When we remove ourselves from the hustle and bustle of the world and go to the wilderness, as Jesus frequently did, and draw near to Him, we will find Him and **know** Him. If we stop and take time seek Him while we work in the garden, wonder at the sunrise, stroll in the park, hike in the mountains, walk along the seashore or by a lake—early when no one else is around—He will be there waiting for us, to show us the wonders and majesty of His handiworks, and to reveal Himself to us. " Proverbs 8:17 "I love those who love me, and those who seek me find me." This favorite old hymn speaks to us of this truth.

In the Garden

I come to the garden alone,
While the dew is still on the roses,
And the voice I hear, falling on my ear,
The Son of God discloses.
And He walks with me, and He talks with me,
And He tells me I am His own,
And the joy we share as we tarry there,
None other has ever known.

He speaks, and the sound of His voice,
Is so sweet the birds hush their singing,
And the melody that He gave to me,
Within my heart is ringing.

Chapter 4: Knowing God Through Observation

And He walks with me, and He talks with me,
And He tells me I am His own,
And the joy we share as we tarry there,
None other has ever known.

I'd stay in the garden with Him,
Tho' the night around me be falling,
But He bids me go, thro' the voice of woe,
His voice to me is calling.
And He walks with me, and He talks with me,
And He tells me I am His own,
And the joy we share as we tarry there,
None other has ever known.

Isaiah 66:2 "For My hand made all these things, Thus all these things came into being," declares the LORD "But to this one I will look, To him who is humble and contrite of spirit, and who trembles at My word.'"

Psalm 19:1 "The heavens are telling of the glory of God; and their expanse is declaring the work of His hands."

Psalm 95:5 "The sea is His, for it was He who made it, And His hands formed the dry land."

Isaiah 43:13 "Surely My hand founded the earth, And My right hand spread out the heavens; When I call to them, they stand together."

STOP Believing in God! Know Him

Job 12:10 "In whose hand is the life of every living thing, and the breath of all mankind?"

Isaiah 40:12 "Who has measured the waters in the hollow of His hand, and marked off the heavens by the span, and calculated the dust of the earth by the measure, and weighed the mountains in a balance and the hills in a pair of scales?"

Isaiah 41:19-20 ""I will put the cedar in the wilderness, the acacia and the myrtle and the olive tree; I will place the juniper in the desert together with the box tree and the cypress, that they may see and recognize, and consider and gain insight as well, that the hand of the LORD has done this, and the Holy One of Israel has created it."

John 1:3 "Through him all things were made; without him nothing was made that has been made."

Job 12:7-10 "But ask the animals, and they will teach you, or the birds in the sky, and they will tell you; or speak to the earth, and it will teach you, or let the fish in the sea inform you. Which of all these does not *know* that the hand of the LORD has done this? In his hand is the life of every creature and the breath of all mankind."

Psalm 96:11-12 "Let the heavens rejoice, let the earth be glad; let the sea resound, and all that is in it. Let the fields be jubilant, and everything in them; let all the trees of the forest sing for joy."

Chapter 4: Knowing God Through Observation

Romans 1:20 "For since the creation of the world God's invisible qualities—his eternal power and divine nature—have been clearly seen, being understood from what has been made, *so that people are without excuse.*"

Psalm 104:24-25 "How many are your works, LORD! In wisdom you made them all; the earth is full of your creatures. There is the sea, vast and spacious, teeming with creatures beyond number—living things both large and small."

God reveals Himself very clearly through His creation, so there really is no acceptable excuse for anyone to not *know* Him.

STOP Believing in God! Know Him

The varied and rich profusion with which God had clothed His world!
(Thomas Guthrie, 1803-1873)

"As we looked down on the pleasant scene, we were astonished at the varied and rich profusion with which God had clothed His world.

Nature, like Joseph, was dressed in a coat of many colors—gray, black and yellow lichens clad the rock.

The glossy ivy, like an ambitious child, had planted its foot on the crag, and, hanging on by a thousand arms, had climbed to its stormy summit.

Mosses, of hues surpassing all the colors of the loom, spread an elastic carpet around the gushing fountain.

The wild thyme lent a bed to the weary, and its perfume to the air.

Heaths opened their blushing bosoms to the bee.

The primrose, modesty shrinking from observation, looked out from its leafy shade.

At the foot of the weathered stone, the fern raised its plumes, and on its summit the foxglove rang his beautiful bells; while the birch bent to kiss the stream, as it ran away laughing to hide itself in the lake below, or stretched out her arms to embrace the mountain ash and evergreen pine.

Chapter 4: Knowing God Through Observation

By a very slight exercise of imagination, in such a scene one could see Nature engaged in her adorations, and hear her singing, 'The earth is full of the glory of God! How manifold are Your works, O Lord God Almighty! In wisdom You have made them all.'

Insects—as well as angels, the flowers that spangle the meadow--as well as the stars that spangle the sky, the lamp of the glowworm—as well as the light of the sun, the lark that sings in the air—and the seraph that is singing in Heaven, the thunders that rend the clouds—or the trumpet that shall rend the tomb—these and all things else, reveal God's attributes and proclaim His praise!"

"Let everything that has breath praise the Lord!" Psalm 150:6

Chapter 5: Knowing God Through Inquiry

"The LORD is near to all who call on him, to all who call on him in truth."
Psalm 145:18

"In everything by prayer and supplication, with thanksgiving, let your requests be made known unto God"
Philippians 4:6

"So Saul died for his trespass which he committed against the LORD, because of the word of the LORD which he did not keep; and also because he asked counsel of a medium, making inquiry of it, and did not inquire of the LORD. Therefore He killed him and turned the kingdom to David the son of Jesse."
1 Chronicles 10:13-14

Chapter 5: Knowing God Through Inquiry

"For the shepherds have become stupid And have not sought the LORD; Therefore they have not prospered, And all their flock is scattered." Jeremiah 10:21

This is what happens when we do not inquire of God and go off following our own foolish minds and wills. We are stupid creatures—our flocks will be scattered and we will not prosper. Instead, we should follow David's lead, and inquire of God about everything. The more we inquire of Him, the more He answers us, and the more intimately we come to *know* Him.

2 Samuel 2:1 "Then it came about afterwards that David inquired of the LORD, saying, 'Shall I go up to one of the cities of Judah?' And the LORD said to him, 'Go up' So David said, 'Where shall I go up?' And He said, 'To Hebron.'"

1 Samuel 23:2 "So David inquired of the LORD, saying, 'Shall I go and attack these Philistines?' And the LORD said to David, 'Go and attack the Philistines and deliver Keilah.'"

1 Samuel 30:8 "David inquired of the LORD, saying, 'Shall I pursue this band? Shall I overtake them?' And He said to him, 'Pursue, for you will surely overtake them, and you will surely rescue all.'"

2 Samuel 5:19 "Then David inquired of the LORD, saying, 'Shall I go up against the Philistines? Will You give them into my hand?' And the LORD said to David, 'Go up, for I will certainly give the Philistines into your hand.'"

STOP Believing in God! Know Him

2 Samuel 5:23 "When David inquired of the LORD, He said, 'You shall not go directly up; circle around behind them and come at them in front of the balsam trees.'"

1 Samuel 22:10 "He inquired of the LORD for him, gave him provisions, and gave him the sword of Goliath the Philistine."

Whenever David faced a trial, especially with his enemies, he always asked to know God's will, and each time he inquired of the LORD, the LORD graciously gave him a clear and definite answer. All the stories in the Bible "were written down for our instruction" Romans 15:4. God did not just respond to inquiries of His people in the Old Testament—He still clearly responds to His children today, we only need to ask.

It pleases God when we ask His will in all areas of our life. If we are faced with any situation where we are not clear on what the next best step is, we should immediately stop and inquire of Him. He knows exactly what we should do, and He will tell us if we ask. When we inquire, our path is made straight. "Trust in the LORD with all your heart and do not lean on your own understanding. In all your ways acknowledge Him, and He will make your paths straight. Do not be wise in your own eyes; fear the LORD and turn away from evil. It will be healing to your flesh and refreshment to your bones." Proverbs 3:5-7.

Matthew 7:7 "Ask and it will be given to you; seek and you will find; knock and the door will be opened to you. For everyone who asks receives; he who seeks finds; and to him who knocks, the door will be opened.

Chapter 5: Knowing God Through Inquiry

Psalm 34:4 "I sought the LORD, and He answered me, and delivered me from all my fears."

Jeremiah 29:13 "You will seek Me and find Me when you search for Me with all your heart."

Psalm 37:4 Take delight in the LORD; and He will give you the desires of your heart.

Isaiah 26:8 "Thou doest keep him in perfect peace, whose mind is stayed on thee, because he trusts in thee."

1 John 5:14-15 "This is the confidence we have in approaching God: that if we ask anything according to his will, he hears us. And if we *know* that he hears us—whatever we ask—we *know* that we have what we asked of him." We have to *know* that God hears us and *know* that we have what we asked of Him—there is no *believing* in it, only *knowing*.

1 Chronicles 16:11 "Look to the LORD and his strength; seek his face always."

Jeremiah 29:12 "Then you will call on me and come and pray to me, and I will listen to you."

James 5:13 "Is anyone among you in trouble? Let them pray. Is anyone happy? Let them sing songs of praise."

STOP Believing in God! Know Him

Proverbs 15:8 "The LORD detests the sacrifice of the wicked, but the prayer of the upright pleases him."

Psalm 17:6 "I call on you, my God, for you will answer me; turn your ear to me and hear my prayer."

Psalm 141:2 "May my prayer be set before you like incense; may the lifting up of my hands be like the evening sacrifice."

Matthew 7:11 "If you, then, though you are evil, know how to give good gifts to your children, how much more will your Father in heaven give good gifts to those who ask him!"

Romans 8:26 "In the same way, the Spirit helps us in our weakness. We do not know what we ought to pray for, but the Spirit himself intercedes for us through wordless groans."

God makes it very clear throughout His Word that He desires us to inquire of Him, ask Him, seek Him—and make sure while we are at it that we praise Him, acknowledge and thank Him for His perfect answers, loving kindness and tender mercies towards us.

Chapter 6: Knowing God Through Relationship

"The righteous cry out and the Lord hears them; he delivers them from all their troubles. The Lord is close to the broken-hearted and saves those who are crushed in spirit. The righteous person may have many troubles, but the Lord delivers him from them all."
Psalm 34:17-19

"But those who hope in the Lord will renew their strength. They will soar on the wings like eagles; they will run and not grow weary, they will walk and not be faint."
Isaiah 40:31

"Be strong and courageous. Do not be afraid or terrified because of them, for the Lord your God goes with you; he will never leave you nor forsake you."
Deuteronomy 31:6

STOP Believing in God! Know Him

When we *know* God, we are secure in our relationship with Him. We *know* He has everything under control. We *know* He loves and cares for us, we *know* we are His children, we *know* He showers us with loving kindness and tender mercies. We *know* He has redeemed us from the pit and that we will be with Him through eternity. He gives us peace and joy and comfort. He supplies our every need. He shelters us, protects us and hides us under His wing. There is no greater relationship we could have or ask for in life. We love, praise and exalt Him, and if we are walking closely with Him, He is our last thought before we drop off to sleep, He is our first thought as we wake in the morning, and He is there with us all through the night and day.

"Do not be anxious about anything, but in every situation, by prayer and petition, with thanksgiving, present your requests to God. And the peace of God, which transcends all understanding, will guard your hearts and your minds in Christ Jesus." Phillippians 4:6-7

"Humble yourselves, therefore, under God's mighty hand, that he may lift you up in due time. Cast all your anxiety on him because he cares for you." 1 Peter 5:6-7

"Peace I leave with you; my peace I give you. I do not give to you as the world gives. Do not let your hearts be troubled and do not be afraid." John 14:27

"Surely the righteous will never be shaken; they will be remembered for ever. They will have no fear of bad news; their hearts are steadfast, trusting in the Lord. Their hearts are secure, they will have no fear; in the end they will look in triumph on their foes." Psalm 112:6-8

Chapter 6: Knowing God Through Relationship

"But God demonstrates his own love for us in this: while we were still sinners, Christ died for us." Romans 5:8

"But you, Lord, are a compassionate and gracious God, slow to anger, abounding in love and faithfulness." Psalm 86:15

"For I am convinced that neither death nor life, neither angels nor demons, neither the present nor the future, nor any powers, neither height nor depth, nor anything else in creation, will be able to separate us from the love of God that is in Christ Jesus our Lord." Romans 8:38-39

"What, then, shall we say in response to these things? If God is for us, who can be against us? He who did not spare his own Son, but gave him up for us all—how will he not also, along with him, graciously give us all things?" Romans 8:31-32

"Trust in the Lord with all your heart and lean not on your own understanding; in all your ways submit to him, and he will make your paths straight." Proverbs 3:5-6

"And we know that in all things God works for the good of those who love Him, who have been called according to his purpose." Romans 8:28

"So do not fear, for I am with you; do not be dismayed, for I am your God. I will strengthen you and help you; I will uphold you with my righteous right hand." Isaiah 41:10

STOP Believing in God! Know Him

Octavius Winslow (1808 –1878)

"Our gospel came to you not simply with words, but also with power, with the Holy Spirit and with deep conviction." 1 Thessalonians 1:5

"The religion of the Lord Jesus is valuable only as its power is experienced in the heart. In this respect, and in this only, it may be compared to the physical sciences, which, however ingenious in structure, or beautiful in theory—yet, if not reduced or reducible to purposes of practical use, are of little worth. It is so with the truth of Jesus.

The man of mere taste may applaud its external beauty, the philosopher may admire its ethics, the orator may admire its eloquence, and the poet may admire its sublimity—but if the Spirit of God does not take His own truth, and impress it upon the heart, as to the great design of its revelation—it avails nothing.

What numbers there are who rest in the mere 'theory' of Christianity! But as a practical principle—they know nothing of it. As a thing experienced in the heart—it is a hidden mystery to them. They speak well of it as a religious system; they believe its Divinity, and even defend its doctrines and extol its precepts—yet make no approaches towards a personal and practical obedience to its claims. In a word, they know nothing of repentance towards God, and faith towards our Lord Jesus Christ. It will surely appear to a spiritually-enlightened mind, a subject of vast and solemn importance that this delusion should be exposed—that this foundation of sand should be undermined—and that the absolute necessity of experimental religion, as necessary to an admission within the kingdom of glory, be strenuously and scripturally enforced."

The words Octavius Winslow wrote back in the late 1800's are as true today as they were then—maybe moreso, because we are now nearer to the kingdom of glory. He was one of the foremost evangelical preachers of the 19th Century in England and America. We desperately need more preachers like him today. You can find more teachings like this if you visit the site www.gracegems.org.

Chapter 7: Knowing God Through Praising Him

"My mouth is filled with Your praise And with Your glory all day long."
Psalm 71:8

Chapter 7: Knowing God Through Praising Him

The word "praise" appears approximately 250 times in the Bible. The word "pray" appears over 300 times. There is good reason for that. God is telling us the benefits of both, because through both, we come to **know** Him. The more we praise Him, the more His Spirit expands inside of us, until we cannot contain it, and the more we **know** and love Him.

Begin each day praising God before you open your eyes in the morning, and your day will be blessed.

Psalm 103 "Bless the LORD, O my soul; and all that is within me, bless his holy name! Bless the LORD, O my soul, and forget not all his benefits, who forgives all your iniquity, who heals all your diseases, who redeems your life from the Pit, who crowns you with steadfast love and mercy, who satisfies you with good as long as you live so that your youth is renewed like the eagle's. The LORD works vindication and justice for all who are oppressed. He made known his ways to Moses, his acts to the people of Israel.

The LORD is merciful and gracious, slow to anger and abounding in steadfast love. He will not always chide, nor will he keep his anger for ever. He does not deal with us according to our sins, nor requite us according to our iniquities. For as the heavens are high above the earth, so great is his steadfast love toward those who fear him; as far as the east is from the west, so far does he remove our transgressions from us. As a father pities his children, so the LORD pities those who fear him. For he knows our frame; he remembers that we are dust. As for man, his days are like grass; he flourishes like a flower of the field; for the wind passes over it, and it is gone, and its place knows it no more. But the steadfast love of the LORD is from everlasting to everlasting upon those who fear him, and his righteousness to children's children, to those who keep his covenant and remember to do his commandments. The LORD has established his throne in the heavens, and his kingdom rules over all. Bless the LORD, O you his angels, you mighty ones who do his word, hearkening to the voice of his word! Bless the LORD, all his hosts, his ministers that do his will! Bless the LORD, all his works, in all places of his dominion. Bless the LORD, O my soul!"

Revelation 5:12 "In a loud voice they sang: 'Worthy is the Lamb, who was slain, to receive power and wealth and wisdom and strength and honor and glory and praise!'"

Revelation 5:13 "Then I heard every creature in heaven and on earth and under the earth and on the sea, and all that is in them, singing: 'To him who sits on the throne and to the Lamb be praise and honor and glory and power, for ever and ever!'"

Revelation 7:12 "Amen! Praise and glory and wisdom and thanks and honor and power and strength be to our God for ever and ever. Amen!"

Revelation 19:1 "After this I heard what sounded like the roar of a great multitude in heaven shouting: 'Hallelujah! Salvation and glory and power belong to our God, ...'"

Chapter 7: Knowing God Through Praising Him

Revelation 19:5 "Then a voice came from the throne, saying: 'Praise our God, all you his servants, you who fear him, both small and great!'"

Ephesians 1:3 "Praise be to the God and Father of our LORD Jesus Christ, who has blessed us in the heavenly realms with every spiritual blessing in Christ."

Ephesians 5:19-20 "Speak to one another with psalms, hymns and spiritual songs. Sing and make music in your heart to the LORD, always giving thanks to God the Father for everything, in the name of our LORD Jesus Christ."

1 Thessalonians 5:16-18 "Rejoice always, pray continually, give thanks in all circumstances, for this is God's will for you in Christ Jesus."

Psalm 9:1-2 "I will praise you, O LORD, with all my heart; I will tell of all Your wonders. I will be glad and rejoice in you; I will sing praise to your name, O Most High."

Psalm 13:6 "I will sing to the LORD, for he has been good to me."

Psalm 16:7 "I will praise the LORD, who counsels me; even at night my heart instructs me."

Psalm 19:1 "The heavens declare the glory of God; the skies proclaim the work of his hands."

Chapter 8: Knowing God Through Jesus

"For God so loved the world that He gave His only begotten Son, that whoever believes in Him should not perish but have everlasting life. For God sent the Son into the world, not to condemn the world, but that the world might be saved through him."

John 3:16-17

Chapter 8: Knowing God Through Jesus

As we read the New Testament scriptures, we come to **know** God in the most lovely, intimate and personal way, through His Son, Jesus, the Word who became flesh. John 1:14 "The Word became flesh and made his dwelling among us. We have seen His glory, the glory of the one and only Son, who came from the Father, full of grace and truth." Everything that Jesus said and did during His time on earth was pure and beautiful, perfect and precious. He is one with God, so through Him, we know God. John 1:1 "In the beginning was the Word, and the Word was with God, and the Word was God."

Hebrews 1:3 "He reflects the glory of God and bears the very stamp of His nature, upholding the universe by the word of His power. When He had made purification for sins, He sat down at the right hand of the Majesty on high,"

Matthew 5:6 "Blessed are those who hunger and thirst for righteousness, for they shall be satisfied." That is how we should seek to **know** God—we should hunger and thirst after Him.

Luke 10:21-22 "In that same hour He rejoiced in the Holy Spirit and said, 'I thank thee, Father, Lord of heaven and earth, that thou hast hidden these things from the wise and understanding and revealed them to babes; yes, Father, for such was Your gracious will. All things have been delivered to Me by My Father; and no one knows who the Son is except the Father, and who the Father is except the Son *and anyone to whom the Son chooses to reveal Him.*'" Thus, if we want to **know** Him, we must lay aside all pride in

STOP Believing in God! Know Him

our earthly intelligence and come to him as children, in simple trust, and ask Him to reveal Himself to us.

If we want God to reveal Himself to us, Jesus said in John 14:21, "He who has My commandments and keeps them, he it is who loves Me; and he who loves Me will be loved by My Father, and I will love him and will reveal Myself to him." There is a special, intimate love that is reserved for those who obey Him, and it is only to those in this close loving trusting relationship, that He reveals more of Himself. As David wrote in Psalms 25:14 "The secret of the Lord is for those who fear Him, and He will make them know His covenant."

Jesus is not referring to the Ten Commandments given to Moses. He is talking about the commands He gave us:

Jesus was asked: "Teacher, which is the greatest commandment in the Law?" Jesus replied: 'Love the Lord your God with all your heart and with all your soul and with all your mind.' This is the first and greatest commandment. And the second is like it: 'Love your neighbor as yourself.' All the Law and the Prophets hang on these two commandments." Matthew 22:36-40

The additional commands of Jesus include:

"So in everything, do to others what you would have them do to you, for this sums up the Law and the Prophets." Matthew 7:12

Chapter 8: Knowing God Through Jesus

"And when you stand praying, if you hold anything against anyone, forgive him, so that your Father in heaven may forgive you your sins. But if you do not forgive, neither will your Father who is in heaven forgive your sins." Mark 11:25-26

"You should not be surprised at my saying, 'You must be born again.'" John 3:7. Jesus is referring to our spiritual rebirth through the indwelling of the Holy Spirit.

"Remain in me, and I will remain in you. No branch can bear fruit by itself; it must remain in the vine. Neither can you bear fruit unless you remain in me." John 15:4. When we invite Jesus into our heart to become our Lord and Savior, the Holy Spirit and Christ Spirit takes up residence in us, and we in Him. Jesus uses a grapevine as an analogy of our relationship with Him.

"You are the light of the world. A city on a hill cannot be hidden. Nor do men light a lamp and put it under a bushel, but on a stand, and it gives light to all in the house. Let your light so shine before men, that they may see your good works and give glory to your Father who is in heaven.'" Matthew 5:14-16

"Settle matters quickly with your adversary who is taking you to court. Do it while you are still with him on the way, or he may hand you over to the judge, and the judge may hand you over to the officer, and you may be thrown into prison." Matthew 5:25

STOP Believing in God! Know Him

"If your right eye causes you to sin, gouge it out and throw it away. It is better for you to lose one part of your body than for your whole body to be thrown into hell. And if your right hand causes you to sin, cut it off and throw it away. It is better for you to lose one part of your body than for your whole body to go into hell." Matthew 5:29-30. Jesus obviously is not telling us to cut off body parts, but He is commanding us to remove from our lives anything that cause us to sin.

"But I tell you, Do not swear at all: either by heaven, for it is God's throne; or by the earth, for it is His footstool; or by Jerusalem, for it is the city of the Great King. And do not swear by your head, for you cannot make even one hair white or black. Simply let your 'Yes' be 'Yes,' and your 'No,' 'No'; anything beyond this comes from the evil one." Matthew 5:34-37

"You have heard that it was said, 'Eye for eye, and tooth for tooth.' But I tell you, Do not resist an evil person. If someone strikes you on the right cheek, turn to him the other also." Matthew 5:38-39

"And if someone wants to sue you and take your tunic, let him have your cloak as well. If someone forces you to go one mile, go with him two miles. Give to the one who asks you, and do not turn away from the one who wants to borrow from you." Matthew 5:40-42

"You have heard that it was said, 'Love your neighbor and hate your enemy.' But I tell you: 'Love your enemies and pray for those who perse-cute you, that you may be sons of your Father in heaven. He causes his sun

Chapter 8: Knowing God Through Jesus

to rise on the evil and the good, and sends rain on the righteous and the unrighteous.'" Matt 5:43-45

"Beware of practicing your piety before men in order to be seen by them; for then you will have no reward from your Father who is in heaven." Matthew 6:1

"And when you pray, do not be like the hypocrites, for they love to pray standing in the synagogues and on the street corners to be seen by men. I tell you the truth, they have received their reward in full. But when you pray, go into your room, close the door and pray to your Father, who is unseen. Then your Father, who sees what is done in secret, will reward you. And when you pray, do not keep on babbling like pagans, for they think they will be heard because of their many words. Do not be like them for your Father knows what you need before you ask Him. This, then, is how you should pray: 'Our Father in heaven, hallowed be your name, your kingdom come, your will be done on earth as it is in heaven. Give us today our daily bread. Forgive us our debts, as we also have forgiven our debtors. And lead us not into temptation, but deliver us from the evil one.' For if you forgive men when they sin against you, your heavenly Father will also forgive you. But if you do not forgive men their sins, your Father will not forgive your sins.'" Matthew 6:9-15

"When you fast, do not look somber as the hypocrites do, for they disfigure their faces to show men they are fasting. I tell you the truth, they have received their reward in full." Matthew 6:16

STOP Believing in God! Know Him

"Do not store up for yourselves treasures on earth, where moth and rust destroy, and where thieves break in and steal. But store up for yourselves treasures in heaven, where moth and rust do not destroy, and where thieves do not break in and steal. For where your treasure is, there your heart will be also." Matthew 6:19-21

"Therefore I tell you, do not worry about your life, what you will eat or drink; or about your body, what you will wear. Is not life more important than food, and the body more important than clothes? Look at the birds of the air; they do not sow or reap or store away in barns, and yet your heavenly Father feeds them. Are you not much more valuable than they?" Matthew 6:25-26

"But seek ye first the kingdom of God, and his righteousness; and all these things shall be added unto you." Matthew 6:33

"Therefore do not worry about tomorrow, for tomorrow will worry about itself. Each day has enough trouble of its own." Matthew 6:34

"Do not judge, or you too will be judged. For in the same way you judge others, you will be judged, and with the measure you use, it will be measured to you." Matthew 7:1-2

"Do not give dogs what is sacred; do not throw your pearls to pigs. If you do, they may trample them under their feet, and then turn and tear you to pieces." Matthew 7:6

Chapter 8: Knowing God Through Jesus

"Ask and it will be given to you; seek and you will find; knock and the door will be opened to you." Matthew 7:7

"Then the King will say to those on his right, 'Come, you who are blessed by my Father; take your inheritance, the kingdom prepared for you since the creation of the world. For I was hungry and you gave me something to eat, I was thirsty and you gave me something to drink, I was a stranger and you invited me in, I needed clothes and you clothed me, I was sick and you looked after me, I was in prison and you came to visit me.'" Matthew 25:34-36

"Enter through the narrow gate. For wide is the gate and broad is the road that leads to destruction, and many enter through it. But small is the gate and narrow the road that leads to life, and only a few find it." Matthew 7:13-14. All these commands of Jesus are narrow gate commands—we cannot obey them if we are wandering the broad road of the world.

"Watch out for false prophets. They come to you in sheep's clothing, but inwardly they are ferocious wolves." Matt 7:15

"He called his twelve disciples to him and gave them authority to drive out evil spirits and to heal every disease and sickness." Matthew 10:1. We have been given spiritual power and authority by Christ through the indwelling of the Holy Spirit, and we are expected to use it, as we are directed—not shy away and say: "I cannot do that!" On our own we cannot, but through the power of Him dwelling in us, nothing that we are called to do is impossible.

STOP Believing in God! Know Him

"Heal the sick, raise the dead, cleanse those who have leprosy, drive out demons. Freely you have received, freely give." Matthew 10:8 (These may seem extreme, and we probably do not believe we encounter many dead people to raise, lepers to cleanse or demons to drive out in our daily lives; but in fact we do. We encounter the sick in spirit and the spiritually dead all the time. Those who are outcasts of the world, such as the homeless, are often treated like lepers, and Satan and his demons do still exist—they did not become extinct when we entered the "age of enlightenment"—and are alive, well and thriving. On demons or Satan in general, when you encounter them, all you have to do is "resist the devil, and he will flee from you." James 4:7. It is really as simple as saying: "In Jesus' Name, I command that you depart from here." It is really much more dangerous to deny their existence than to command them to depart.

"See that you do not look down on one of these little ones. For I tell you that their angels in heaven always see the face of my Father in heaven." Matthew 18:10

"But you are not to be called 'Rabbi,' for you have only one Master and you are all brothers. And do not call anyone on earth 'father,' for you have one Father, and he is in heaven. Nor are you to be called 'teacher,' for you have one Teacher, the Christ. The greatest among you will be your servant. For whoever exalts himself will be humbled, and whoever humbles himself will be exalted." Matthew 23:8-12. In this chapter, Jesus is teaching against elitist behavior. This is directed at the Rabbis themselves, not to the followers, which does not win Him any popularity among the Jewish leaders. His command against calling leaders "father" is to prevent the elitist practice of giving high status to men which is due only unto God. The Catholic Church openly defies this command; however all Christian organizations that use exalting titles for their leaders are culpable. "I will not show partiality to any person or use flattery toward any man." Job 32:21.

"If your brother sins against you, go and show him his fault, just between the two of you. If he listens to you, you have won your brother over. But if he will not listen, take one or two others along, so that 'every matter may be established by the testimony of two or three witnesses.' If he refuses to listen to them, tell it to the church; and if he refuses to listen even to the church, treat him as you would a pagan or a tax collector,'" Matt 18:15-17. Many people misinterpret this scipture and believe that Jesus is saying they should be cast out. In fact, if you look at those Jesus associated with—tax collectors, prostitutes, all manner of sinners and unsavory people by the standards of the Pharisees—that is obviously not what he means. "Later, as Jesus was dining at Matthew's house, many tax collectors and sinners came and ate with Him and His disciples. When the Pharisees saw this, they asked His disciples, 'Why does your Teacher eat with tax collectors and sinners?' On hearing this, Jesus said, 'It is not the healthy who need a doctor, but the sick.'" Matthew 9:10-12. He was saying that they should be loved, nurtured and invited to dinner, so that they might repent and be forgiven. You do not encourage a brother to repent by casting him out.

"Have faith in God," Jesus answered. I tell you the truth, if anyone says to this mountain, 'Go, throw yourself into the sea,' and does not doubt in his

STOP Believing in God! Know Him

heart but believes that what he says will happen, it will be done for him. Therefore I tell you, whatever you ask for in prayer, believe that you have received it, and it will be yours.'" Mark 11:22-24

"Which of these three, do you think, proved neighbor to the man who fell among the robbers? He said, 'The one who showed mercy on him.' And Jesus said to him, 'Go and do likewise.'" Luke 10:36-37

"My command is this: Love each other as I have loved you." John 15:12

"The Lord Jesus, on the night He was betrayed, took bread, and when He had given thanks, He broke it and said, 'This is My body, which is for you; do this in remembrance of Me.' In the same way, after supper He took the cup, saying, 'This cup is the new covenant in My blood; do this as often as you drink it, in remembrance of Me.'" 1 Corinthians 11:23-25

"Be merciful, just as your Father is merciful." Luke 6:36

"Therefore go and make disciples of all nations, baptizing them in the name of the Father and of the Son and of the Holy Spirit, and teaching them to obey everything I have commanded you. And surely I am with you always, to the very end of the age." Matthew 28:19-20

"If you love me, you will obey what I command." John 14:15

"You also must be ready, because the Son of Man will come at an hour when you do not expect him." Luke 12:40

Chapter 9: Knowing God Through the Holy Spirit

"As for you, the anointing which you received from Him abides in you, and you have no need for anyone to teach you; but as His anointing teaches you about all things, and is true and is not a lie, and just as He has taught you, you abide in Him."

1 John 2:27

STOP Believing in God! Know Him

While we yet remain in the world, it is the Holy Spirit who is the most important One in our coming to *know* God, and in our transformation into the image of Christ.

John 16:13 "But when He, the Spirit of truth, comes, He will guide you into all the truth; for He will not speak on His own initiative, but whatever He hears, He will speak; and He will disclose to you what is to come."

Ezekiel 36:27 "I will put My Spirit within you and cause you to walk in My statutes, and you will be careful to observe My ordinances."

John 14:26 "But the Helper, the Holy Spirit, whom the Father will send in My name, He will teach you all things, and bring to your remembrance all that I said to you."

Matthew 10:19-20 "But when they hand you over, do not worry about how or what you are to say; for it will be given you in that hour what you are to say. 'For it is not you who speak, but it is the Spirit of your Father who speaks in you.'"

2 Corinthians 6:16 "Or what agreement has the temple of God with idols? For we are the temple of the living God; just as God said, 'I WILL DWELL IN THEM AND WALK AMONG THEM; AND I WILL BE THEIR GOD, AND THEY SHALL BE MY PEOPLE.'"

Romans 8:11 "But if the Spirit of Him who raised Jesus from the dead dwells in you, He who raised Christ Jesus from the dead will also give life to your mortal bodies through His Spirit who dwells in you."

Romans 8:9 "However, you are not in the flesh but in the Spirit, if indeed the Spirit of God dwells in you But if anyone does not have the Spirit of Christ, he does not belong to Him."

Romans 8:15 "For you have not received a spirit of slavery leading to fear again, but you have received a spirit of adoption as sons by which we cry out, 'Abba! Father!'"

Galatians 5:22 "But the fruit of the Spirit is love, joy, peace, patience, kindness, goodness, faithfulness, gentleness, self-control; against such there is no law."

Galatians 5:18 "But if you are led by the Spirit, you are not under the Law."

Just as the Father and the Son have many names which describe and set forth their character and work, so also the Holy Spirit has names which describe His character and work.

THE HOLY SPIRIT

Luke 11:13 "If you then, who are evil, know how to give good gifts to Your children, how much more shall your heavenly Father give the Holy Spirit to those who ask Him?" Rom.1:4 "... according to the Spirit of holiness..." The Spirit Himself is holy and produces holiness in us.

STOP Believing in God! Know Him

THE SPIRIT OF GRACE

Hebrews 10:29 "How much worse punishment do you think will be deserved by the man who has spurned the Son of God, and profaned the blood of the covenant by which he was sanctified, and outraged the Spirit of Grace." As the executive of the Godhead, the Spirit confers grace. To resist the Holy Spirit is to close off all hope of salvation.

THE SPIRIT OF BURNING

Matthew 3:11, 12 "… He shall baptize you with the Holy Spirit, and with fire." Isaiah 4:4 "when the Lord shall have washed away the filth of the daughters of Zion and cleansed the bloodstains of Jerusalem from its midst by the spirit of judgment and the spirit of burning." Matthew 3:11 "I baptize you with water for repentance, but he is who coming after me is mightier than I, whose sandals I am not worthy to carry; he will baptize you with the Holy Spirit and with fire. His winnowing fork is in his hand, and he will clear his threshing floor and gather his wheat into the granary, but the chaff he will burn with unquenchable fire." This cleansing, the burning off of the chaff, is done by the Spirit's fire. He burns off the dross in our lives when He enters and takes possession of us.

THE SPIRIT OF TRUTH

John 14:16-17 "And I will pray the Father, and he will give you another Counselor, to be with you forever, even the Spirit of Truth, whom the world cannot receive, because it neither sees him nor knows him; you will *know* him, for he dwells with you, and will be in you." As God is Love, so the Spirit is Truth. He possesses, reveals, confers, leads into, testifies to, and defends the truth. As the Spirit of Truth, he reveals to us the spirit of error. 1 John 4:6 "We are of God. Whoever **knows** God listens to us. By this we know the spirit of truth and the spirit of error."

THE SPIRIT OF LIFE

Romans 8:2 "For the law of the Spirit of life in Christ Jesus has set me free from the law of sin and death." Romans 8:11 "If the Spirit of him who raised Jesus from the dead dwells in you, he who raised Christ Jesus from the dead will give life to your mortal bodies also through His Spirit which dwells in you." The controlling flesh has been deposed, and its place taken over by the Spirit of life.

THE SPIRIT OF ADOPTION (SONSHIP)

Romans 8:14-15 "For all who are led by the Spirit of God are sons of God. For you did not receive the spirit of slavery to fall back into fear, but you have received the Spirit of Sonship. When we cry, "Abba! Father! It is the Spirit Himself bearing witness with our spirit that we are children of God,"

THE SPIRIT OF INTERCESSION

Romans 8:26 "Likewise the Spirit helps us in our weakness; for we do not know how to pray as we ought, but the Spirit Himself intercedes for us with sighs too deep for words. And he who searches the hearts of men knows what is in the mind of the Spirit, because the Spirit intercedes for the saints according to the will of God." We do not know what or how to pray, so the Holy Spirit intercedes for us, to help us. When we are praising God and can find no words in our language sufficient to convey our gratitude, love and adoration of Him, the Holy Spirit knows and intercedes for us. When we are humbling ourselves before God in despair over our lowliness before Him, the Holy Spirit intercedes for us, "with sighs too deep for words".

THE SPIRIT OF WISDOM AND KNOWLEDGE

Ephesians 1:17 "and asking that the God of our Lord Jesus Christ, the glorious Father, may give you a spirit of wisdom and revelation in your *knowledge* of Him." Isaiah 11:2-3 "The Spirit of the LORD will rest on Him, The spirit of wisdom and understanding, The spirit of counsel and strength, The spirit of *knowledge* and the fear of the LORD. And He will delight in the fear of the LORD, And He will not judge by what His eyes see, Nor make a decision by what His ears hear;" 1 Corinthians 2:9 "But, as it is written, 'What no eye has seen, nor ear heard, nor the heart of man conceived, what God has prepared for those who love him,' God has revealed to us through the Spirit. For the spirit searches everything, even the depths of God."

THE SPIRIT OF PROMISE

Ephesians 1:13 "In him you also, who have heard the world of truth, the gospel of your salvation, and have believed in him, were sealed with the promise of the Holy Spirit, which is the guarantee of our inheritance until we acquire possession of it, to the praise of his glory." Acts 2:23 "Therefore having been exalted to the right hand of God, and having received from the Father the promise of the Holy Spirit, He has poured forth this which you both see and hear." The Spirit is the fulfillment of Christ's promise to send the Comforter—He is the promised Spirit. The Spirit also

Chapter 9: Knowing God Through the Holy Spirit

confirms and seals the believer, and assures us that all the promises made to us shall be completely fulfilled.

THE SPIRIT OF GLORY

1 Peter 4:14 "If you are reproached for the name of Christ, you are blessed, because the spirit of glory and of God rests upon you." Glory as used in the Scriptures means divine quality or character. The Holy Spirit is the One who produces godlike character in those who *know* the Lord. 2 Corinthians 3:18 "And we all, with unveiled face, beholding the glory of the Lord, are being changed into his likeness from one degree of glory to another; for this comes from the Lord who is the Spirit."

THE SPIRIT OF GOD, AND OF CHRIST

1 Corinthians 3:16 "Do you not *know* that you are God's temple and that God's Spirit dwells in you?" Romans 8:9 "But you are not in the flesh, you are in the Spirit, if the Spirit of God really dwells in you. Any one who does not have the Spirit of Christ does not belong to him."

While taking my morning devotional walk recently, God placed the Holy Spirit heavily on my heart and mind. I realized that through knowing, loving, praising, exalting and following Jesus, I know, love, praise and exalt my Father. "I and the Father are one"–to know the Son is to know the Father. The Holy Spirit   although I know He is in me, working and speaking through me, guiding me, teaching me, interceding on my behalf, and comforting me in times of trials—was not personally and intimately known to me, as are my Father and Jesus. The acts and workings of the

STOP Believing in God! Know Him

Holy Spirit are so secret and mystical–so much is said of His influence, power and gifts, that we are prone to think of Him as a power, a manifestation or influence of the Divine nature, an unknowable agent rather than a Person. I immediately began praying that He would reveal Himself to me, personally—not as the nebulous, disembodied, impersonal spirit that I had been experiencing. Then I began praising and exalting Him, giving Him glory for the incredible part He plays in my daily walk as a Christian, in my *knowledge* of God and Christ. As I did so, I became overwhelmed with the *knowledge* of Him and just how critically important knowing Him and engaging Him personally on a daily basis truly is.

We all *know* the fruit of the Spirit is love, joy, peace, forbearance, kindness, goodness, faithfulness, gentleness and self-control. We can never truly manifest these fruits without the indwelling of the Holy Spirit. Although people try, no one is able in their human capacity to do other than make a poor show of mimicking the fruits of the Spirit.

The Holy Spirit regenerates us, through the renewing of our mind, so that we can understand things of the Spirit. He indwells us "Your body is the temple of the Holy Ghost which is in you", 1 Corinthians: 6:19. He empowers us for the life and service God has planned for us. The Holy Spirit guides us—"A righteous man's/woman's steps are ordered by the Lord"—when we listen to the Holy Spirit directing our steps, we are always exactly where we need to be, when we need to be there, for God's will (not our own) to be done. He seals us with the assurance of salvation—the Holy Spirit is "the Spirit of adoption" which God puts into our hearts, by which we know, on an intimate, personal level, that we are His children. The Holy Spirit anoints the believer for teaching and **knowledge**, service and consecration. The Holy Spirit is the author and interpreter of the Scriptures, and it is through Him that God's Word comes alive to us, in Spirit and in Truth. Finally the Holy Spirit can be grieved–to refuse any part of our mortal nature to the full sway of the Spirit is to grieve Him. If we continue to grieve Him, that grief turns into vexation. We do not want to vex the Holy Spirit!

There is a difference between being indwelled by the Spirit, and being filled with the Spirit. All Christians, those who have accepted Christ as their Lord and Savior, receive the baptism of the Holy Spirit at which time He indwells us; however, not all are Spirit-filled. We need to know, acknowledge and interact with the Holy Spirit, and give Him free reign in our lives. Although it may not be necessary, I am in the habit of asking for an overflowing of the Holy Spirit on a daily basis, and He is never stingy with Himself if we ask.

In these times, we all need to be Spirit-filled believers, and to come into a closer personal relationship with Him who gives us all the power and tools we need to live victorious lives in Christ Jesus. Without His power, we are ineffective vessels, unable to become sons and daughters in whom our Father is well pleased, or to truly know and love Him. Worse, we may not be hearing what the Holy Spirit is telling us, which is critical in these days. We need to be Spirit-filled so that our eyes and ears are fine-tuned to immediately see and hear what He is showing and speaking to us. If He

STOP Believing in God! Know Him

says: "Go here or go there now!" we need to be hearing Him and doing what He is telling us, without question or hesitation. The Holy Spirit is amazing! Get to know Him and let Him do His work in and through you.

I made the mistake a year or so ago of delaying after receiving the Holy Spirit's clear, emphatic command, saying: "Go Now!" I was still saved from what was coming, but not without suffering consequences due to my delay, consequences I would not have suffered if I had acted immediately, as He directed me. It was a very good lesson for me. When He speaks now, I listen and act immediately, and do not allow my own willful, foolish "rational" mind to get in His perfect way. I pray we all learn this lesson without having to suffer unpleasant consequences in the process, especially coming into the times of tribulation.

"If the Holy Spirit is a Divine Person and we know it not, we are robbing a Divine Being of the love and adoration which are His due. It is of the highest practical importance whether the Holy Spirit is a power that we, in our ignorance and weakness, are somehow to get hold of and use, or whether the Holy Spirit is a personal Being, who is to get hold of us and use us. It is of the highest experimental importance. Many can testify to the blessing that came into their lives when they came to know the Holy Spirit, not merely as a gracious influence, but as an ever-present, loving friend and helper." Dr. R. A. Torrey (1856-1928)

Chapter 10: What We Do Believe

We believe in faith unto salvation. Once we have believed, we then *know*.

STOP Believing in God! Know Him

We believe in faith unto salvation. Once we have believed, we then *know*.

Romans 10:9-11 "that if you confess with your mouth, 'Jesus is Lord,' and believe in your heart that God raised Him from the dead, you will be saved. 'For with your heart you believe and are justified, and with your mouth you confess and are saved.' It is just as the Scripture says: 'Everyone who believes in Him will not be put to shame.'"

Galatians 3:6-9 "So also Abraham 'believed God, and it was credited to him as righteousness.' Understand, then, that those who have faith are children of Abraham. Scripture foresaw that God would justify the Gentiles by faith, and announced the gospel in advance to Abraham: 'All nations will be blessed through you. So those who rely on faith are blessed along with Abraham, the man of faith.'" This is where faith comes into the equation—we must first in faith believe, before we can *know*.

John 12:37-43 "Even after Jesus had performed so many signs in their presence, they still would not believe in him. This was to fulfill the word of Isaiah the prophet: 'Lord, who has believed our message and to whom has the arm of the Lord been revealed?' For this reason they could not believe, for again, Isaiah says: 'He has blinded their eyes and hardened their hearts, so they can neither see with their eyes, nor understand with their hearts, nor turn—and I would heal them.' Isaiah said this because he saw Jesus' glory and spoke about him. At the time, even among the leaders, many believed in him, but because of the Pharisees they would not openly acknowledge their faith for fear they would be put out of the synogogue—for they loved

Chapter 10: What We Do Believe

human praise more than praise from God." He is speaking here of people who were standing before Him and seeing Him perform many signs in their presence. Earlier in the chapter, Jesus says: 'Father, glorify Thy name.' Then a voice came from heaven, 'I have glorified it, and I will glorify it again.' The crowd standing by heard it and said that it had thundered. Other said: 'An angel has spoken to him.' Jesus answered, 'This voice has come for Your sake, not for mine.'" Even after seeing the signs and hearing God's voice, they still did not believe in Him. Obviously they did not disbelieve in His person, because He was known and physically standing before them; they did not believe that He was the Messiah because their hearts were hardened.

Acts 16:30-32 "Then he brought them out and asked, 'Sirs, what must I do to be saved?' They replied, 'Believe in the Lord Jesus and you will be saved, you and your household.' Then Paul and Silas spoke the word of the Lord to him and to everyone in his house." Some people get confused by this scripture, believing it is saying that if the head of a household accepts Christ, then his whole family is saved. In this recounting, the message of salvation was proclaimed to the jailer and his whole household, and it was believed by the jailer and his whole household—and as the jailer professed his faith by being baptized, so did the others in his household.

While we are still of the World and living in sin, we must *in faith believing* accept that Jesus Christ is the Son of God, that he was crucified, died, was buried and then resurrected for the redemption of our sins, so that we might become adopted children of God, and be saved from the eternal damnation

STOP Believing in God! Know Him

of hell. Once we have in faith believed and accepted, we are then indwelled with the Holy Spirit and the Spirit of Christ, so we no longer need to believe—we now *know*.

That is the only time we believe; that is the only time we: "accept (something) as true—feel sure of the truth of; or to hold (something) as an opinion—think or suppose." We step out in faith believing something we do not know, so that we may *know*.

Now that we *know* God, we stand firm in our implicit belief in His Word, as we would believe what was written in a letter from a trusted friend, but with a substantially more solid belief—the friend, no matter how trusted and loved could embellish details and leave out important information. God tells us all we need to know to *know* Him, and there is no deception in Him, so we *know* what He tells us is absolute Truth. There is no one and no thing on earth that we can stand on with that conviction of belief, because we *know* God.

Chapter 12: What We Come to Know

" For this reason I bow my knees before the Father, from whom every family in heaven and on earth is named, that according to the riches of his glory he may grant you to be strengthened with power through his Spirit in your inner being, so that Christ may dwell in your hearts through faith—that you, being rooted and grounded in love, may have strength to comprehend with all the saints what is the breadth and length and height and depth, and to *know* the love of Christ that surpasses knowledge, that you may be filled with all the fullness of God."
Ephesians 3:14-20

STOP Believing in God! Know Him

Once we have stopped *believing* in God and started *knowing* Him, things begin to change for us in dramatic ways.

The more we *know* Him, the more we desire to know Him more deeply. The more deeply we *know* Him, the greater grows our love for Him. The more we *know* and love Him, the more aware we become of just what vile, loathsome, worthless creatures we are—completely without any redeeming value whatsoever. We realize—as the knowledge of His greatness, His infinite wonder, majesty, beauty, love and grace settles into our aware-ness—just how contemptible, of less value than dust, we are. We want to crawl under a rock and bury ourselves beneath the worms to hide from the splendor of Him who we cannot look upon because of His greatness, His awesome power, His infinite amazing Grace and Love poured out on us. We recognize the unspeakable repulsiveness of our pride and vanity—the utter despicable arrogance in which we have attempted to exalt ourselves above Him, ignore Him, deny Him, refuse to acknowledge and trust Him, and to place our insignificant wills and foolish faith in ourselves over Him.

We now begin to *know* the magnitude of the incredible gift Jesus gave when He offered up His life for us so that we might be redeemed. We begin to *know* the dreadful, horrendous place He willingly allowed Himself to be lowered to when He took our sins upon Himself—in the process being sep-arated from the Father. How horrible that was for Him—words cannot possibly express. He went to Hell for us, so we would not have to go there, even though that is exactly where we deserve to be. We cannot help but weep at the realization—tears of intense joy, and tears of utter despair over our sinfulness and unworthiness. We now comprehend the simplicity and the magnitude of what Jesus came to teach us.

Chapter 11: What We Come to Know

We now comprehend what Paul was saying to us in Ephesians 3:14-21 "For this reason I bow my knees before the Father, from whom every family in heaven and on earth is named, that according to the riches of his glory he may grant you to be strengthened with power through his Spirit in your inner being, so that Christ may dwell in your hearts through faith—that you, being rooted and grounded in love, may have strength to comprehend with all the saints what is the breadth and length and height and depth, and to *know* the love of Christ that surpasses knowledge, that you may be filled with all the fullness of God.

Now to him who is able to do far more abundantly than all that we ask or think, according to the power at work within us, to him be glory in the church and in Christ Jesus throughout all generations, forever and ever. Amen."

We suddenly *know* that we have been drawn into the love life of God the Father, Christ the Son and the Holy Spirit—being rooted and grounded in love, we are comprehending the breadth and length and height and depth of the love of Christ that surpasses knowledge, and are becoming filled with the fullness of God—and we are so incredibly humbled by that knowledge.

Habakkuk 2:14 "For the earth will be filled with the *knowledge* of the glory of the LORD, as the waters cover the sea."

Conclusion

The word **believe** or **believeth** appears approximately 285 times in the Bible. The word **know** or **knowledge** appears approximately 950 times. From that alone, we must conclude that God is much more interested in our **knowing** than in our **believing**. "The fear of the Lord is the beginning of wisdom, and **knowledge** of the Holy One is insight." Proverbs 9:10.

True knowledge of God comes down to obeying the stipulations of his covenant. It is expressed in living conformity to his will. The opposite of knowledge is not ignorance, but rebellion. 1 Samuel 15:22-23 "Samuel said, 'Has the LORD as much delight in burnt offerings and sacrifices as in obeying the voice of the LORD? Behold, to obey is better than sacrifice, and to heed than the fat of rams. For rebellion is as the sin of divination, and stubbornness is as iniquity and idolatry Because you have rejected the word of the LORD, He has also rejected you from being king.'"

If we are not experiencing as close and intimate a relationship with God as we desire, it is because we are not seeking Him with a true hunger and thirst, and we are rebelling against Him by not obeying Him, so He is not revealing Himself to us. "Draw near to God and He will draw near to you." He has clearly told us how it works. Psalm 42:1 "As a deer longs for a stream of cool water, so I long for you, O God."

The list of commands that Jesus gave us in the New Testament, included in Chapter 8, may seem like a long list, but it really all boils down to: "Love the Lord your God with all your heart and with all your soul and with all your mind." If we do that, everything else is automatic. You cannot love God with all your heart, soul and mind and not love your neighbor as yourself, or do unto others as you would have them do unto you. You

Conclusion

cannot Love God with all your heart, soul and mind and not want to be in His Word, praying to Him, singing songs and praising Him constantly. You cannot love God with all your heart, soul and mind and not have complete faith and trust in Him, and the desire to do His will in all areas of your life.

It is a very simple and ever upward moving spiral, but we have to start—we have to jump in. When we read His Word, pray and praise Him, we get to *know* and love Him, which makes us want to read His Word, pray and praise Him more, which makes us *know* and love Him more, which makes us want to read his Word, pray and praise Him even more, which makes us *know* and love Him even more. And all the while, as we are drawing nearer and nearer to Him, He is drawing nearer and nearer to us, until He envelopes us, and we are in Him and He is in us, as Christ is in Him and us and He is in Christ, as the Holy Spirit is in Them and He is in us. We become an intimate part of the amazing love life of the Trinity— and it just keeps getting better into eternity.

So Stop believing in God—*Know* Him, and join in the amazing love life He is calling us into. We cannot get there by *believing* in Him, only by *knowing* Him—for to *know* Him is to love Him.

About

Ellen Lefavour accepted Jesus Christ as her Lord and Savior in 1970. Over the years, she has wandered off the narrow path and through the wide gate of the world. He was ever beside her, and although she was not always acknowledging Him as He deserves, she always knew He was there.

Now is God's time and He is calling all of His in, waking those who have fallen asleep, and claiming those who were chosen to be His from the beginning of creation—the lines are being drawn. God is calling for that intensity of a close walk with Him, so that all of His might be fully prepared for the times that are coming, and conformed into the image of Our Lord. He is calling us to stop *believing* in Him and *know* Him.

Ellen lives in Gloucester, MA, where she paints and writes as God leads her, witnessing for Christ, and watching and waiting for His Glorious Appearing. "Behold, I am coming soon..." Rev. 22:12

Please visit www.hobbithousestudio.com to see and learn more about the paintings and books God has been leading Ellen to bring into being for His glory and purpose.

Also, please visit www.godsmorning.live, a blog providing daily teachings and a platform for followers of Christ to share their knowledge and love of God the Father, Jesus Christ, His Son and our Salvation, and the Holy Spirit who teaches, guides and comforts us.

www.ingramcontent.com/pod-product-compliance
Lightning Source LLC
Chambersburg PA
CBHW060158070426
42447CB00033B/2205